Selected Duets

for TROMBONE
or BARITONE

Published in Two Volumes:

VOLUME I (Easy-Medium)

• VOLUME II (Advanced)

Compiled and Edited

by H. VOXMAN

RUBANK®

HAL•LEONARD®
CORPORATION
7777 W. BLUEMOUND RD. P.O. BOX 13819 MILWAUKEE, WI 53213

PREFACE

Duet playing affords the student the most intimate form of ensemble experience. The problems of technic, tone quality, intonation, and ensemble balance are brought into the sharpest relief. Careful attention must be given to style as indicated by the printed page and as demanded by the intangibles of good taste.

Mastery of the art of duet playing leads easily and naturally to competent performance in the larger ensembles. The numerous works included in this volume have been selected for the purpose of introducing the instrumentalist to the finest in two-part ensemble literature and acquainting him with a diversity of musical forms and expressions.

H. Voxman

●

CONTENTS

Duetto III

DIETTER

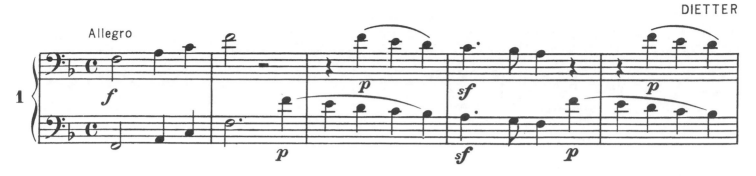

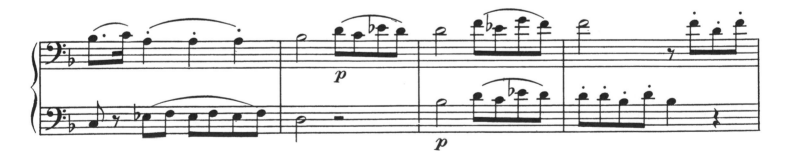

Duetto VI

PLEYEL-BLUME

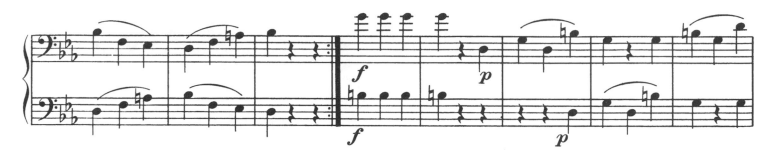

Alla marcia

Sonata II

CROFT
(1678 - 1727)

Adagio

Allegro [in four]

Allegro moderato

E. KRAKAMP

Allegro

6 *mf*

Fine *p*

mf

mf

f

D.C. al Fine

Minuetto

BRAUN

[Allegretto]

7

Prestissimo

CORNETTE

8

D.C. al ⊕

CODA

Vivace

Minuet

18th Century

10

Sonata

FINGER
(ca 1660- ?)

Allegro (in four)

Grave (in three)

Presto (in four)

Spiritedly

18th Century

12

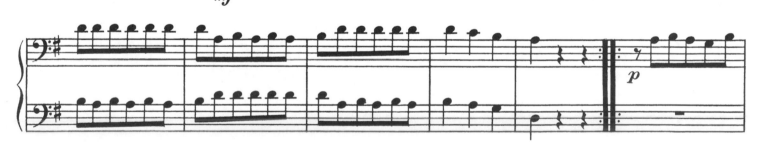

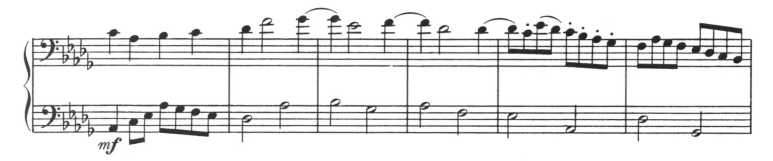

Gigue

BOISMORTIER

Allegro

15

Allemanda
(Sonata VI)

BOISMORTIER

Sonata II, Op. 40

BOISMORTIER

Gavotte

HAAG

March

HAAG

Seventh Lesson

MONTECLAIR

Vivace
Practice also in B Major

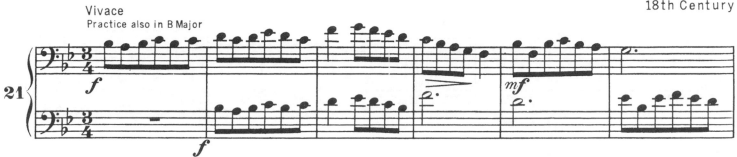

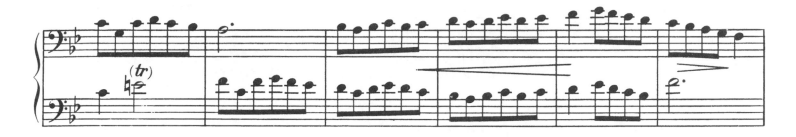

22

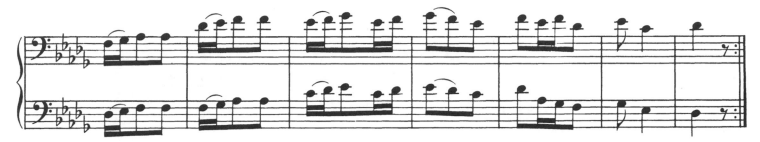

Caccia
(Hunting Song)

18th Century

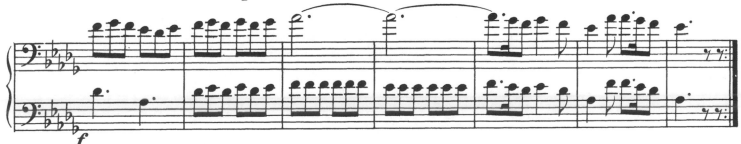

Aria

HANDEL

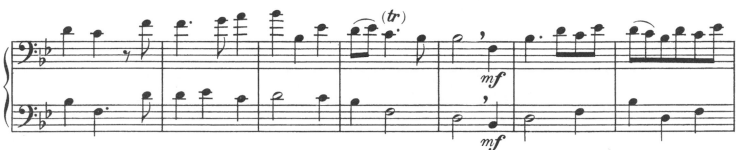

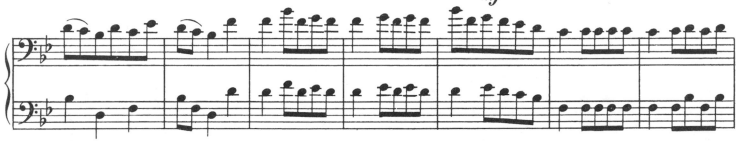

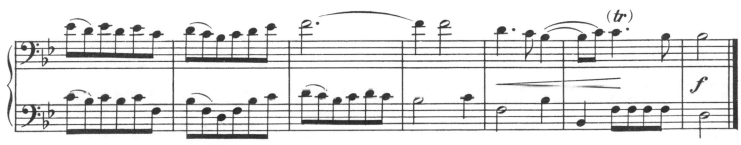

GEMINIANI

Adagio

26

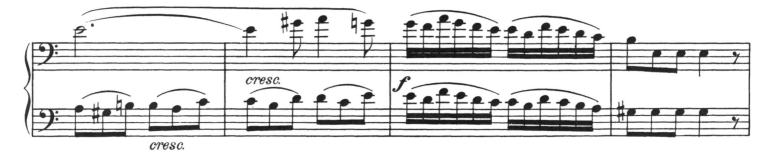

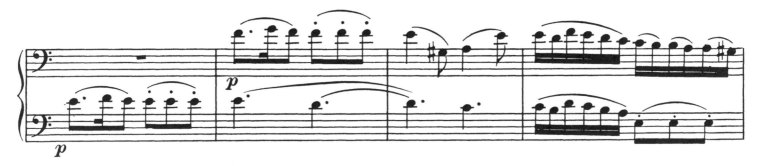

Leveillé

Gaily

AUBERT

D. S. al Fine

Tambourin

AUBERT

BORGHI

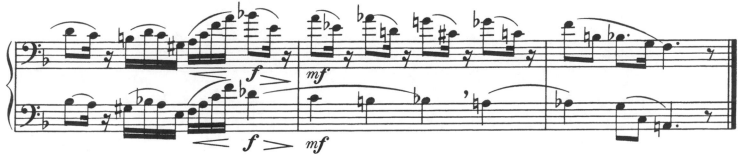

Andante mosso (♪ = 152)

30

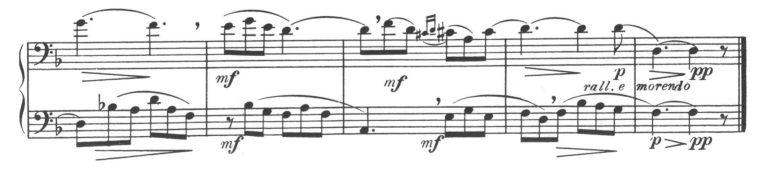

Allegro vivace

31

44

POPP

Gigue

33

Moderato

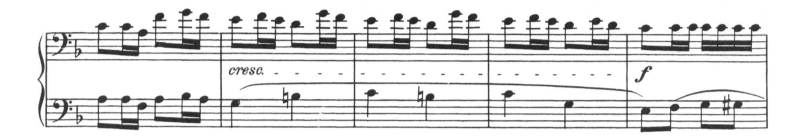

34 *pp*

cresc. - - - - - - - - - - - - - - - - *f*

Fine

mf

CLODOMIR

Moderato

35

50

CLODOMIR

Allegretto

36

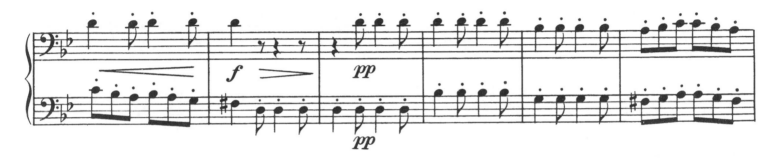

CLODOMIR

Tempo di menuetto

38

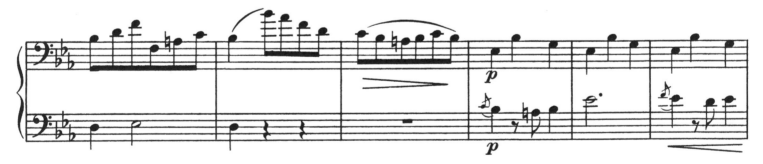

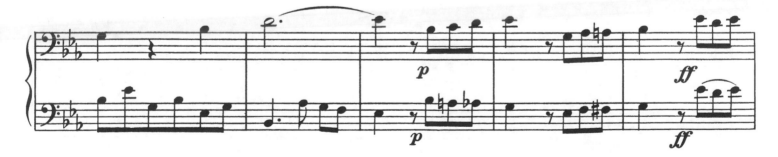

Duo Concertant No.1

VOBARON

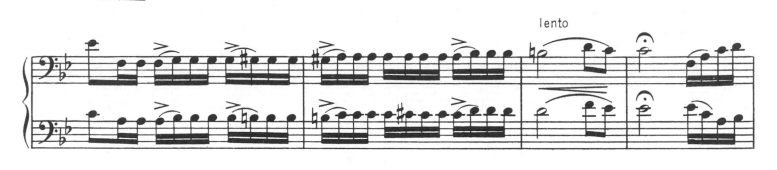

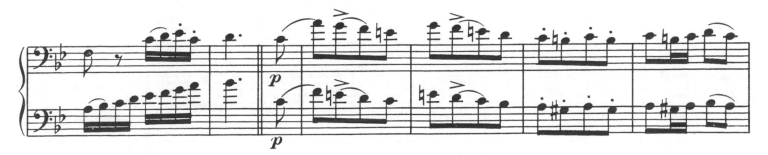

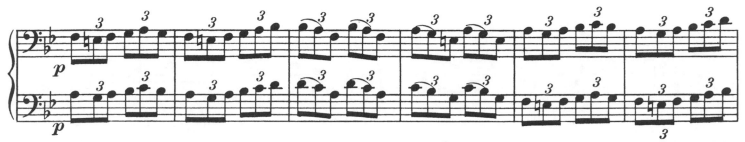

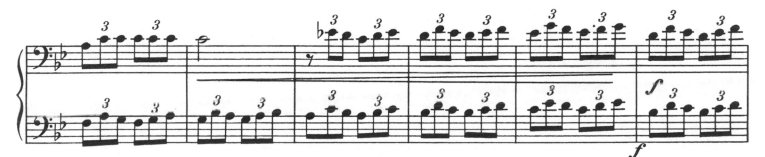

Polonese

Moderato

PETSOLD

Allegro moderato

42

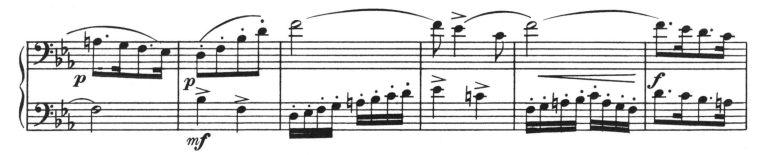

43

Andante con dolore

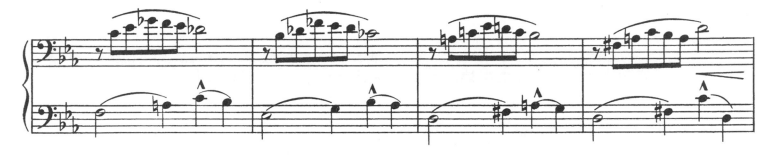

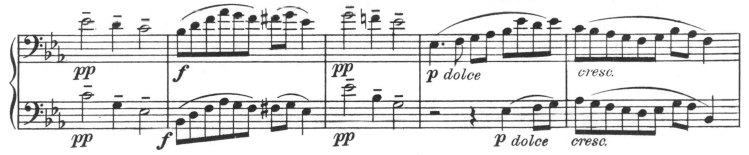

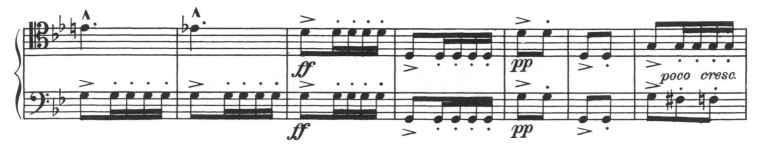

Allegro vivo con leggierezza

BLAZHEVICH

46

Concert Duet No.10

BLAZHEVICH

Concert Duet No.19

BLAZHEVICH